*is that a bruise
or a tattoo?*

sean burn

is that a bruise or a tattoo?

Shearsman Books

First published in the United Kingdom in 2013 by
Shearsman Books
50 Westons Hill Drive
Emersons Green
BRISTOL
BS16 7DF

Shearsman Books Ltd Registered Office
30–31 St. James Place, Mangotsfield, Bristol BS16 9JB
(this address not for correspondence)

www.shearsman.com

ISBN 978-1-84861-294-5

Contents

ACKNOWLEDGEMENTS

work first appeared in the following:
blue and yellow dog ('pohádka'); *blueprintreview* 24 ('scarif'); *libus berlin* ('steal this loneliness' ii); *hanging johnny* ('catwalk' and 'butcher shimmies'); *pinhole camera* 4 ('ravenswing'); *otoliths* published *is that a bruise or a tattoo* sequence july 2010; *liminal* was published in *shearsman* (april 2011)

parts of 'when a child unseen encircles rough woods my mind' were first exhibited as poster-poems for the annual art invasion of cumbria co-ordinated by fold gallery, 2005. the final section was made by sean into a poetry film, premiered at crosstalk video art festival, budapest, june 2010. it was first published by *fire* magazine 2011

'buds have spoken b(l)ack'—performance text with integral sound-scape was premièred as sound installation at carlisle arts festival, 2009.

'bastilles englan'—an interdisciplinary performance involving text / soundscape / visual poetry and live art was premièred at platform 00000008 and has since toured internationally. the text was first published in *sunfish* # 5.

this book is dedicated to miki z

catwalk down a tongue old albion

(after linder, pretty *girl no. 1*)

multiple brokens
brighting around
adze and mirrors
no particular
your catwalk
down a tongue
old albion this
immaculate
end torn-under
graspgrease
—a run(a)way
beleaguered
catcalleyes
lies and thighs
leer and cheer
stomachs in
chest out
mark births excise
from cameras glaze
glory holes
more than a
swallow good
kiss night
right over edges
think brownfield
ledge and legs
open eye closed
rape fantasy aint
daubed across
trading standards
don't disturb

how this meat might
always to carve
wanna into this eat

forging new new
by hook or
perfumed
the eternal
incise rust
weld us well
us tight
feedback-slow-
sigh-trajectories
boudoirs eventing
evening views
slow choke
whose thin-sliced
on the news?
even broadsheets
are downsized and
shaking their
porn-baron
wingding
behind another
grinning re-erection
is the premiers
former daughter
just-legal yet?
black through white
why do we
have sex 'with'
but make love 'to'?
least theres no
mistaking
where hardcore sat

some private
cutting us out
soft has limpid eyes
how do cow moo
oh leaders wives
spread your
inflationary tease
the net tightens
bleeding hearts
bingeing on all
chairs-and-men
the last one out
please turn
and the rest?
drastic halves
plastic arse
more florists of unthink
measuring con-con
census of hard-ons
liturg that dull familiar
our wrists arent
what they once

upsuck, unstuck
get real, get bloody
rages-grasp
around fleshdom
hinged on
squeeze harness
no lengths none
cant stop looking
chubby adult libraries
grab a string flickerings
uphold the honour
bruisings hapless execute

the most cage inside
different skins
like nothing before
this little went to market
and this little too
and this and this
while that little suckling
wrote the whole
business plan

all vinegar petals
honey wires
and to the easy
ever more remote
scrap scarred scrips
what makes me sick

for all the silence you are?

for all the silences you are

jezebelofthewaters

water companys thievery of these parts
cloudbomb pipe-burst or just slow drip
sip lascivious pilgrimages to from of jezebels
silently sweating a floodbloodied valley
kitting out carafe of table deicide
kind-of liquortender and the lions lie down
a new chapter of blue-blue etceteras
all lipslicks truthpicks upsticks
and shower me dark deep
offmessages of *your call is precious*
have please unique pin number to hand
the blood granita flush falls just off-tap
oh how the water bankers laugh

and outrages a label jezebel wears skin-tight
thirty percent sweat-lycra reminding
if canals a street then rivers a broadway
cruising and oozing so sip the tall glass yeah
their encyclopedic cleansing via rich voice
neurotypical furred tea ever warned warmed
ready battened battered and downheavy
how the water bankers laugh
their tenderizing pearlchapped peal
playing footsie of pump and fizz
taps and turnpipes, standpipes and standbys
cutoffs and goodbyes, turncoats hosing wells
through one-liner lonelinesses sewer corruptible
through multiple lease greasebacks
barebacked at years turning

    perfecting excess
don't iceberg poor, don't watersteel

just lowspit mid-hiss reive
for all you threatening to spill
and over and over in on s-s-some
water-borne droit de seigneur coursing
the rest go screw without lube
countless counties awash
pale flooding, huge numb lies
of coming knowledge-o
throw down, throwing down
walking on water, the walking of water
seducing to the depths of liquid light
down drownpipes of memory, memories of
the floodclear valleys of north-torn, solway to kielder
the company knows best, company knows best, company knows
so arrest the water, timetable the water
castrate, perforate, score a perfect
frustrate now and prostrate—just how dya
calculate the water bill?   after all

waters still multilingual multi-angled and viva bisexual
great fat beats sucked from the uncountable teat
slipside reverb of jezebel sighs never-to-be
untamed newborn blueskies wetdreaming
down the last siren wailproudwater
virtualwater optimistwater loudbruisewater
big and hard and heavy, la-la underground
mamabuddhas seduction wars to the depth
to the unfathomable s-s-suck the clear h2o snake
oh you jezebelofthewaters dam-blue skirts
lifting outside the slippy drainmain/s of love

perrierslaves, volvic voyeurs, crispclean malvern slappers,
        ballygowan tarts, carreg sloggers,
bouteille bleu sluts, pellegrino sans everything
                and the badoits up for rent, again

how you distort the line, the lie, the dribbling lie
pooling downwards to restless tv symphonies
postcolonial nil by mouth buzz overheadunderfoot
the flight no fight kind of we are doing everything
leading the world, pissing you now, gold gates open
oh youre pissing us now, pissing us and how
the companies flowerbeds, their immaculate quiet art
drip-drip-dripping saltstuff into our direct debit mouths
leave us thirsty, leave us wanting more, we want more
want it now, try through dryfried prism, heavysiege
drownlung suck, the kiss of reducing, seducing, our bottle to dry

my butcher shimmies a rectum
inside the warm duvet cow

105 106 108
and this in the shade
an unbearable waiting
coming in under radars
all neonburger and pizza
all waffle and southern syrup
all tutti-fruity and vomiting
an all screaming all dancing
all-cabaret the untied states dreaming
blow me now baby oh yeah the greed
creaming chelseas buns of honey
randy valentines and cruella de clinton licking
lip-synch lewinsky screaming desert foxy
milf astride a cruise to die for
how about 0898 senate sluts pumping white
how about fist-twisting bowels
your house of unrepresentatives
chief justices blown until
theyre smoke ringing and singing
this ones beyond politics and skin
and can we have our bomb back please

how about the blast of mingus monk and ayler
of harvey milk kathy boudin and angela davis
their blast the beat the beat

hei-ho hei-ho—our father, tart dreaming
split screen liver spleen ribs
for what we're about to deceive
it could-of been mind fist blue
it could-of been plus full colour

can you believe in out in
and all for 64,000 rightwing dollars
6 million oil-pumping and rocketing
coke future tax free and low fat
reporting your fabulous bitching birth
all viagra, voodoo and sleazenation viva dot visa
salute the holywood nazis all singing all dancing
ve have vays of making you bambi
rifles for jesus—this ones a k k k 47
the barrelstock all sanded down
of rebelheart and magnolia
already swung in the wind
and above all if the glove don't fit wear it
lost and found oh yeah baby
meat thieving king of swingers
hand me down your ruby slippers
your ruby slippers now

but the blastbombs of carla bley etta james ma rainey the beat
the beat going on

fire deep in dollar zero
ham and pineapple deserts
gritting technicolor teeth
pilgrim mothers hung out to dry
the schmaltzdisney vein
mined for anaesthetic
all cocktail aesthetics
icepicking through the cryofreeze
goof guys, you flame-resist cretins
throbbing the new olympics
cock-bobbing the synchronized bush beat
hundred metre peanut dash
quarter mile blow-off porkonautics
long-distance club-class endurance-slop-shop

following the leader, following the breeders
aerodynamics of shuttles gone spectacular wrong
a generation of kiddies up on nasa porn
science never used to be this much fun
i wanna be like you-u-u
i wanna do ba doo ba boo boo
now we're kerosene dreaming
crackling frequencies of mullah
a fucked fanfare of suck it and see
 the poet rambo don't know, he don't give a
a jazz jive uzi old glory spattered
star strangled and mother of all
we'll be back

but the blast bombs of carlos williams tennessee williams john
coltrane clifford brown lawrence ferlinghetti the beat the heat
the heats going on

steal this loneliness

a decayed of performing across this strained continent

i

take me sweet-juiced
with bondage-fruit
acid-lands pimping smile
pitching you grease
screwing you with sand
somewhere over pill-pop   or
squaring the best demotic offer
creep again please
our ave stolen   in
grubby union boxers
add sequins, nil by psychosis
sneak too much mouth
throw or outgrow us
stress the great placid grab
this islands flense
breaking our face
on fist this cage now
the unlock heave-cleaved
bound/hounded   in
porkbarrel operettas
folks tra-la-la folios
1979 /1997
anagrams, whatever
each generations consumed
its last sad-salad
oh yeah where
the rich get duller as
the poor get strapped

and everywhere
the numbers switch

of redfists burning
insensitivity shrines
controlled manuscripts
your willed-i-content
a right to blow me where?
this necropolis assumes
    used-car cyclones
cluster-bomb steakholders
genetically modified tartlets
water outsourcers   skin execs
as bones chord-call thrillseeks
typefields appointed confessors
the whole parole now
so monstrous exploded
a hard believed relief clause
half-relieved belief clause
of what bonefield
soubrettes who quit
those who have yet
thin-lipped shock-oratorio
no longer this acid-land
is said out-cashed
money cannot
man cease when
his porn gape
his wants cease
him gape no longer
be g(o)od   but end down to luck

ii
rooms obliquely
light hunting the outtake
                the badlands
the coil sprung refuge of bed
the speedway whatever

        mothercity
zone attitudinal
   out of print
keep one step ahead
  disperse libraries

night-times   replace all signs
              one way
i was walking along one day
  one way   walking one day i was
walking one way i was

here i was   look right
fill in the blanks yourself
raise roofbeams
in the fourth time of dying
                    smile

        seduce shadow
burn rift
ride the light show
     the wires closing
lopped outtakes

pause   don't answer (that)
struggle to outpace your monologue
change the word?
offer up faces?

i don't buy it

    no longer dream
this conversation is no
        phantom voice/d
    rosy apple
    file corrupted

black swan
      royalties
thrashing the water
     lines of
  salt ribs ship

descend the staircase
diagnose melancholia/s
      green doors
monsieur monsieur?
this is not in the script

brave empire of doubt
lick the burglar
search dark water
trigger suppressed
buglers all

tête a tête
oxygen corona
ascend the dark step
endless walking
translator of the line

iii

line of spine, lie of the land
heel to heel, hand over hand

peninsula dream-arcing chill
edge/s of the rip haemorrhaging

life is no rehearsal
i have bled five lights for you

beat the disintegrate
borders ravine control

darkmeats gold, this salting
twice my duty, half my joy

maw full of fire as tongue
teasing arse and equally defiant

bend us over the edge
a cracked handful of notes

shot through with space
haunting this relentless place

where we live-love-fuck
torn between glory-delay

last-light-echo   blade spilling rust
you heard of codeine like, ever?

the teeth-cracking truth of
balancing nose on ends of face

this evidence-seam bridging my ideal
thumbnail marks smoothed away

work / don't work - cross / don't
mass-critical
                    your leather mind
of drag, mines the dawn howling

out-led i'm snow all turned to piss
empires chained to edges of chaos

skin-carnival tailing to silence
butchers reading the map better

your fear is fear itself

iv

livestock metallic
within systems lowing
the gob-less, the unstop
celluloids crackling
the darkness-chord
a shuffling waltz
all within this
stutter-call

spotlights
the sound of keys
finally putting down
for the night-split
ruins don't just
happen but may
actively bribe
the axe fall

shoemakers
bend right
in circle dance
sound the fuel
furthest point
klaxoning
the hollowed laugh
keep most of all circles
armament of your will

wrestle asylum
mash medicine
lick arse like dog
if only we could reach
water rucks paper

the pursing of lips
as we are forced to
chew paper
that pulpy
cloying pap
desperate
to get taste out

barbwire heart
in slow pan
window bricked
uncut silhouettes
retune to silence
a march of ache
all that exact
of moment, writing
the same poem
conducting the
same wars
all of our lives

v

citizens of the rearview
we've all had the dream
but some of us lived
that duality fucking
lubricated ballet
of need / greed
riding the volume
what matters is
going beyond
robbed honey
of nicotine walls
a pint of runaway
silky scratchcards
paying for it oddball
oh the petrol of night
    shock the slab
risk whats going down
unbreathe one exactly
      for the road
good can still shock
screensaver reading
steal this loneliness

steal this loneliness
    swallow up
protocols of silence
plagiarise guts
candyfloss locks
everywhere the
eyes fuck and fuel
off-clock, locked in
trust every inch
order a compromise

tongues deform shadow
shiny with insolence
the beauty in a coil of wire
contract each lunge
outside this heaving
stun to aftermath
rags click together
this episode before

refuse sentences
manoeuvre glass
grab at wings mirror
this at least reads true
staggering like never
don't that road again
      melody wank
blank notes
the following options
landscape-dotted
flail with the tongues
affairs con-versations
this lawless night
shenanigan in spasm
fold the smoke in two
crave dark big gulps
the blueprints all sickle
hammerings and
forever reading
still these lonelinesses

liminal *(for dancer tim rubidge)*

                              always
this rocks cumulative rotations

wind drag across bones
tongue becomes fight

the mirror azure
to depths undreamt

unarmed by sun
fist of light tightens

time brittles
with each slow breath

amplify light
bird without roots

a flightless tree
fight and upside

and concrete pages
encourage tears

bloody page spill
lives unread

whose out of step?
turn the book around

feather necessity, flesh
being flesh is torn or worn

at dusk and dust recall
lips skipped in stutter-rhyme

this sweet day, between yourself
and child-song pures

*

outreaching to the broken last, trying to? not so much bridge as
milky-span, toe the line, keep within channels, don't jerky-dance
some magenta-bleed, eyes glide from hand, try some slammer,
for crying out. winged, but then who is? and who is lidless sweat,
ever kneeling, supplication in deep-sunk inhibiting machine

*

light swelters
swells in gesture
jester you
apply match
urging shelter
in airs rare shell
oxygen unfurling
kindling tricks
and again
trip/ripped
ripe flailings
back slam
coincidencing
the spilt up
rouged flight
necessary
as splitting light
pained air lines

reverb blooding
extraordinaire
this arabesques
inked in stutter
mining somewhere
around dawn

spark eyes fruit lung
from tree of body
no sudden gusts
giddying toward
unusual shoulderings
destroy hard data
write vast surfaces
stare unlocked
saffron wide
border is
borders are
wingfold chained
edges of chaos
fist years, flux us
lung ecstatic
grasp at skybreath
your winged tang
on differing tracks

# of sand red stone i am *(coventry)*

of sand red stone i am
a shell of concrete
echoes of man

of light buttressing the air
as two bronzed figures kneel
tear salt from reddening apertures

and last laugh echoes depart
hide and seek the late light
and falling   and fallen   and peek-a-boo

rough and tumble   horseback rhyme
this is the way the concrete rides
the concrete rides   the ...

of charred timbers
oak preparing to sail without roof
stone red light

to press the flesh
and other fermentings
the upside drum-scars of metal

bet on this   this bête noire
becoming city   and then some
chocolate reparation cake filled

oh you whose inkflow acts up vinegar
calling all hero re-openers
oh how we laugh the antique flesh

down-singing

       skin-deductible

             honey-pages

hurdle shaper	all roman nosed a
handle placer	woman walks the
hopper feeder	tightrope between
neck swager	curb and concrete
hand waxer	her granita lips
procurer of parts	desire length skirt
carton maker	rubbing up against
double stitcher	the crotching
double seamer	flasher-mac gents
double carton tyer	curbed only when
hand stitcher	her stiletto soul
neck placer	raps thin their
fork packer	blank eyed skulls
hand strip	*i'm*
operator	*no in love*
riveter of…	*with*
line quality inspector	*gladioli*
examiner	*theyre so*
end stacker	*stiff*

the whistler of hopes
constructor of legends
scaffolder to the clouds

of this floodquiet floor
their brokeback columns
stone sanded air risen again

these calendars of stone
pulse meditations of
beat beat beat of concrete rights

this prayer-facility is no longer operational
this prayer-hole-in-the-wall is now closed
inhale our all-day everyday tower-blocks

singing   swinging   sighing   swearing
signing how we built this place
brick by bloody brick

glory hallelujah concrete slaves
who will build yous out of this
now our encores cemented firmly in

aching duel ringed road carried away
carriageways underpasses and flyovers
jewel this city no roof but eyeless blue
the lungmeat clouds passing through
phoenix room poppy fantasias scarlet
the bareback streets godiva-face
erased pebble-dashed sand mute
half timbered   three-quarters gone
no face   two-faced   about-face
one way no way please thank you sorry
sort of a   everything for 99 pence
is that the time   theres fish to fry
underpasses to catch my friend, my love, my ducks

godiva plazas for sale for rent for real for ever and ever
no go amen rows of mock tudor street cut timber
throatcutting loss of passage all-queens of
of lies i have been known to sing

angry in the aisle concrete anthems
their ride-a-cock-horse requiems
this city no roof   sailing out

rhythms of this
this rhythm
of   this

ravenswing *(helvellyn)* — *for jeremy hilton*

raven wings the blues above a rock giving finger to red tarn,
      striding edge
i eat baguette welsh-buttered, drink nicaragua fairtrade coffee
watch from wind-hollow the feathering shriek as winged-beat rolls
this is not co-ordinate, not an interstices, not a gridpoint
is as close to perfection as it gets, climbing out above it all
where raven tumbles a switchback shake, shimmies its feathers
reincarnation of elmore james burning his fingers taut up strings
raven slicing air as life depended, in flagrante again and in love
and with each sweetmeat moment, mix your exact beats per minute
your darkest shade, oil slick as, coming in under crackle of radar
truth feathers a reinforced aria, love of wing mediates love of wind
climbing out above it all—romantic or corny—i know, i know
on the other side is thirlmere—the most natural of lake and manmade
and folks washed from under and everywhere stone, stones stitching
      up the land
the lines of road, the lining of reservoir, lines of drystone wall, walling
and penned in fields, in cars, penned in, and two black sheep graze
      united utilities stone
and we tread volunteer-repaved 'permissive paths'—access a privilege
      not a right
walk treeline, bracken line, rough grass, grasses, knotts, pikes, crags
raven now lazying further off, gliding down to something like ten
      bpm
and though place-names mark the shift of language, land marked
      to the passage
of peoples, this palimpsest, i am above the stitch, climbing out
      above it all
—apart from my own breath, but everywhere the seam of stone
stone seaming up the land, the seam of stone stitching up the land
and winds arrow, coiled springs of air and wings flayed, theres an
      energy to it all

ravens night is that pure dark only north, moors, rocks, scar
    can bring
an absence, its not a colour, its a leaching, a bleaching away
raven pearls the ten pence pale moon, bleached so far off, falling
i too have fallen many times, have fucked up, but above all i am
don't belong to the canon of english, of literature, or a cannon of
or some small-arms fire or bayonet or rpg or non-existent wmd of
my north-words are simply me too in experiencing sadness, joy
wondering what its all about, wandering the north, finding how
before owning our own labour, we own our voice, our voices, plural
don't matter whether its printed, spoke, signed, sung, danced,
    txted, performed
set out in form, runs down the page, across the page, to the edge
    or not,
whether its solid inkstone block or spattered, its voice, voices
    becoming
storm, a howl, protest, collision, elisions, harebells of voices,
honeysuckling voices,
these blaeberry of voice, fruit, many flower, hung drop, a collective,
    a lullaby,
the jarrow marchers, the mass trespassers, we march, our voices
    trespass
raven lets out shriek, pure hysteria, a scar, a star, a star, a scar, one
    voice, many voices

buds have spoken b(l)ack

(after lorna graves exhibition, tullie house, carlisle, 2008/9)

have the buds spoken?
spoken black?
have buds spoken?
have buds spoken black?

sleep lack, smile back
heave leaf half smoke
earth-bare firing on up
waters winding on back

have they spoken?
spoken black? those buds
have they spoken
spoken black?

sneak beck beak bell
bark dark, ochre, hock
dig up, unburial
grounds for what?

blood lapse
lap and back-slap
sleek fracture leaking
slack speaking lack

smack! that with
curly or soldier 'c/k'?
budding sky-child
talking back

and chansoning lark-like
how can we, can we be

found if we are not lost?
answer, answer us that

spokes and spoken for
back or black
buds hadnt spoken
hadnt spoken back

beckon sneck
beck bead blood lapse
no bleating just bleed
beat bead back

flood lead neck
to account, counting
calling, no falling, no
falling back

buds have spoken
spoken, spoken back
buds have spoken
buds have spoken b(l)ack

when a child unseen encircles rough wood my mind
(wasdale)

blank moss ignorance
with green sleep lace
that rise and taut fall
steep yearly bloom

by fire and stars
walks with current
lingmell beck tempting
high wrong glad

forgive their sparking
unculled of plough
the air mantling
unprecedent air-shorn

ever-needling beat
parted ages whisper
from mutable respect
whose depths wilding

long flew the fragments
fickle chambering
endless sapphire
breath-cleaved shore

half sky rocky
earth eyes resigned
journey end
struggling to advance

envying throw of clouds
paintflow ignites the
wild crumbled dance
a moist cling-cradle
woods rare cleave
loud as ghosts
reckless own voice
brilliant of years
dark and rare
in unprotect
flood dizzying
ash from
why cages
fluttering that
whatever fruit
maddens wings
struggling loud
mouth negligent
of such speak
whose rib
liquifies synapse
or rip untrue
sweet fusion
sinuous lapse
blue of every
rough broken
in liveliest gleam
cherish the flow
flow the dream

tacitus scribed this archipelago of the edge as warring tribes, crossed swords mark the o.s. maps, battle re-enactments growth industry

not everyone has a novel in them, but lies? now theres a textual art and a half.   sir jeffrey might claim bronze awarded at world lying championships three miles south

was a time before gender re-assignment on the n.h.s. *fee fie foh fum i smell the blood of*—smears of empire pink, sign (on) the dotted line

nosebleeds
the skies of war
r.a.f. cleaving bedrock
our red of before

s.s.s.i's are firing ranges
absurd long campaigns
for preservation of species
so long as theyre no ours

traffickers in shares :
you counted the cost yet
to productivity of all
those two minute silences?

southern psychiatrists
their cream chinos
walk-holidaying
far sides wast water

all this way
to abandon volvic
plastic halos
down creviced scree

rowan berries
fat as red-faced buddhas
come sun or rain
handfuls of dark stain

the secret of blackberries
moon-huge under silver birch

sundew and butterwort
feast on late ringlets, graylings

we don't read
the fractals of this place
wool carded on rock
the potentilla and quartz pace

red admirals at 2,000 feet. less fragile than we imagine that they can bear these dore head cross-winds or is nothing left in wasdale below? either way, childhood saw more butterflies, wasnt that so? now is cubes of mist solidifying to scree, and always this question—where is home? its more longing than belonging on any grid i know

bastilles englan

'its about two years since i was first sent up in this hell and french bastille of english liberty'. john clare

(dis)
late apples   core and all
pips shot out between fingertips
foes imagined   foe-real

(caulder)
belt   laces
belt   laces   please!

(luck)
storm is risin   storm is risin

(dis)
child i gobblin up the late-flowerin
the snapdragon hollyhock sweet-pea

(caulder)
sir? sir! your belt, your laces

(luck)
was the *sirs* did it, they always do
blues fall down like drops of rain

(caulder)
by time you look
synapses have already decided
what you'll see

(all)
gotta draw real line the metaphoric sand

—but here? now?

    (dis)
    and so a thousand pamphleteers
    surround our house

(luck)
your tears   us awake
keepin   kept   nights

    (dis)
    joyful as virginities losin
    tears your two, three, many
    a life-time, lifeline say

        (caulder)
        empty hangers drove just drive me wild
        but mostly i'm glass-half-full kinda

    (dis)
    names dis by the way
    and thats no quote
    a translation rather
    maybe, perhaps
    dis dis dis   dis dis dis

(luck)
storm is risin
blues fall down like drops of rain
stooorm isss riiisin

        (caulder)
        read the signs cant you?
        we're gonna have to render
        sir? sir!

(luck)
singin train station see, barefoot too
couldnt have, they just couldnt
madness that way

(all)
bastilles englan this darkest of dance— this is the way the
madman rides the madman glides the madman slides and down
into the ditch-ditch-ditch

      (dis)
      psycho - psychosis - psychoses - psychotic -
      psychogenic - psychoneurosis - psychonaut -
      psych out and over

(luck)
friction burn down shins
dragged and drugged
us to and through asylumed
slummed lengths their corridors
world-wards   and after
     couldnt stand
          storm is risin
blues fall down like drops of rain

(all)
storms dark dancin - black thorns drop reign - larkness blue
darkness sermons-dis - hedged thunder elides dis - the right
knot, glides dis - burn us down yeah? - dis-flood, dis-glint,
dis-edge - tender render land - asylumed ready frictions forbid
forbid - steal gland dis

      (dis)
      justice?
      just dis

(caulder)
sir? sir!   sir! sir! sir!
assessments - ward rounds - one to ones -
supervisions - on-calls - meds reps - the
endless sodding tea's

(dis)
tease tease
- its a tease-tease-tease!

(luck)
unsleep torch in eyes - outta bed cuppa - meds queue piss - down
lie down - din-dins - lie back - cuppa - meds - pissbed - unsleep -
torch-eyes - outta - meds cuppa piss

pills universal
ills universe
swills and wills
empty this church

(dis)
at least for a while
at last   atlas blast

(caulder)
five milligrams rising ten
ten rising twenty
antipsychotics little r&r
better you for   see?

(all)
agitation, tremor, spasm
painful erections, prolonged erections,
painful and prolonged erections
do not operate machinery,

do not drink, do not breast-feed
etcetera etcetera etcetera

(luck)
checkin under tongue
seein i swallowed
shinin torch right in
like they was csi

ring-ring-a-rosies
a mouth full of
and we all we all we all
fallin down
fallin down

        (caulder)
        circles and circling
        their many and varied walks
        stopstart   startstop
        hug-walls
        segmenting like grapefruits
        boxing
            glacial
                drift
        peacock   constipate   figure-eight

    (dis)
    what the hands do
    where eyes go
    thats what counts

    eye to eye   to eye to eye   to eye to eye to
    until the rift horizons beyond under through

(luck)
wheel-steer   wrapunwrap   sicklehammer
sell-sell-sell chaosconduct windunwindwindin
                until the rift

      (caulder)
      season ends
      pheasants interesting shooting
      wised up after all those near near misses

   (dis)
   night-times
   hoothoot hoot-hootin
   owls down-flyin a closer

(luck)
you never stolen, truly stolen
been truly stolen away?

   (dis)
   a cello could play us one day

      (caulder)
      glass-half-full, like i said

   (dis)
   ten-nine-eight-seven-six
   caught transfixed
   five-four-three-two-one
   theyre never gettin close again

(luck)
best kiss that meaty fist yours bee-sting great bee-stung beastin

(dis)
best kisses my life, lives?
tomorrow yesterday always and all ways

     (caulder)
     first day back after ... late for dash-dash-dot
     ... early-grey too-too hot ... toast
     buttering tie ... mr bump they used to
     but now head-gardener, to say: i garden
     heads

(luck)
and butter-side up
never-never learn
i never-never

     (dis)
     buttercup-buttercup-buttercup!
     the child   hood   game

     (caulder)
     why wait for us to throw back heads
     laugh like executioners?
     always

     (dis)
     wanna know, truly know?
     look to the unruly trees, look

(luck)
wasnt just let sittin floors that ward
was a health and safety see

from wards fire escapes
weeks undressin that silvered birch
- leaf by shimmyin leaf
only thing that would hold my eyes

>(dis)
>trees make us
>but we unmake the tree

>>(caulder)
>>twenty nine days that singular leaf
>>declining red to fall
>>patients - clients - customers?
>>but wheres your focus caulder?
>>never could that trees taxonomy

(all)
a psychiatrist is a psychiatrist is a psychiatrist
but each our psychoses individual unique alone

(luck)
pouf!   hits us like that!
smile, i actually smiled

>>(caulder)
>>the patient was observed, yes, laughing almost
>>safely say they werent experiencing episode that day

(luck)
bog windows this wodge wood jammin - money outrun somewheres
down the pfi - nickin tea-spoon the communal kitchen - toilet
constant four days - and no-one writin up -

(dis)
disafforest - disaggregate - disarticulate - disassemble -
disavow

(luck)
four days spoonin till wodge wood comin free - i'm climbin
out - and nurse-on-fag stare cos i wasnt theirs - runner? more a
waddle, weight-gain of these meds! - tate modern balconys high
enough, only thing i can - miles, so many - shoe-less - blood-
loss - sweat - right in, i fit - actually makin that upper floor but
forgettin, forgettin what to do next

(dis)
disbud - discolour - discompose-discrepant-
disencumber

(caulder)
our reports variance
with your worldview :
care to?

(luck)
this police cell days greyest fry beans bake tea bread ever till
hospitals arsed enough to crash-team down-retrieve their damage
goods

(dis)
disenthral - dismast - disport - dissolute - distal

(luck)
dreamin this ultimate reality: bastilles englan - rival hospitals,
and each with a flop, a nut and a reeeaaall wild-card - camera-
roll, break on out, see how far they/we get/got - prince of
bloodied wales? afghanistan? minister for local communities?
cannot a suitable prize though

(caulder)
must tame the weeds our garden
other the flowers don't reach sun

(luck)
sharp? sharps? us emptyin pockets - flurry-flow, fast-fast-faster,
now and always, leaf-leave-leaves driftin brilliant against your
dirt-desk - stoooorm isssss riiiisen

(dis)
always carry a decent apple
- a russet say

the truth? a truth, leastways

beating their wings on cages, cages

aya eya uiu uaia æeeeo eeu æeee uuaaiia æææeeoeu letters: first
of sainkho namchylaks recordings i heard, years past, and the
sounds, the sound - it physically brought tears - not thought-
up-tears, acts of remembrance, but pain-full, pain-fueled – like
experiments in ultrasound, the 16hz tigers-roar paralysis rather
than sonic-curdlers of war

eu   ee   ua ia oeeu
oyiyooaa   toho tohioyooa

gu ggjjeeeee keiyo o o wu
nnnnnngghhu   aiyeeeeayuiyu

guttural keening we translate
as the wide throat of pain

papa i read your old letter
and suddenly wanted to cry

eich   u eich   eich   ee i o iho
the punching of earthquake

freer than worlds but still birds beating their wings on cages,
cages, the music-haunt, as pained-full, so beauty-powered, her
sort-of there voice and also not. i have danced with her, dance
with her. sat so still i danced so much. keep dancing. keep

eyu aya aiya gheueuuuuuuuuu
aayyeeuu aya ghgghghgh uhuuu

cheeayo aiya   fetid nights
the width of vibrating reeds

ckv cvk cv cv cvkkkkkk-vc-vc free, freer – free-her: the sound of
birds beating their wings on cages, cages   hhvc-h-hhh   vvhhc-
vcch   vv-hhv   v-ch-ghzh   eeo

don't know why or how i survived
our old house blackened with age papa

hhch hh hhch hh hhch gguzheeoo

tongueless cries of devotion
debauchery despair

ultra sound arcing continents
is passions resonance bared

after sainkho namchylak,
esp. *letters* (leo records - cd lr 190)

pohádka *(fairytales)*

čtvrtek

needing cake these parts bohemia and all buildings marzipan /
sneak rear-curlicues - eat and run / these prices the cakes should
come to us / known hunger, want food on me, by me, with /
who hasnt the pizza crustings others leave - their cheese string
licks / now is bulbous as onions storing autumn / bridge under
e55's a candidate for trolls / the largest pop-up book and no
danger of flat / hell to almost smile / eye-smoulder firing up
for her sister - comrade - flame / don't usually believe in happy
endings, but?

pátek

comrade loosely translates as palace / drumsticks   non-stop -
rolled up headlies flashing / follow our yellow-brick roadie / *have
you finished - ja - but also i am finished* / little otik has eaten the
building / unpick mazed rococo featherings / medovníks cake-
crushed -honey uppermost / first slice for sugar-rush, the second
to savour / and as with all the sweetest tooths, pain with the
pleasure (t.b.c.)

sobota

the most interesting folks are non-symmetric? / the warfare most feared! / bass players meta-viral threads from this spore / clubs taken heavy fire / witness the electrification table and history cocktails / theres cutting up rough and then theres cutting up steel / light squeezing eyeballs, rage to bait, confront harness / bread baskets its case to chubbed libraries / go grab a string of flicker and beyond

nedele

whose on little otiks cannonball menu? whose not! / hunting peanut galleria, trout cheeks, interrogated steak, and all non-stop / švejks now hotelier-ier-ier, steam rising chicken-licken-death-metal and afters: little coffins with shipping cream / all hands on duck / whole physiques deformed by heavy playing of spoons

pondelí

semtex is the drinks menu / havel trolley-dollying northbound / don't throw molotovs from train windows / gretel wolfs hans under the chinny, hair-soft / the slaughtering of plums, their ripe-bruise fermenting / which fairytale i'm from, originally— forget st. george and the moneylender / knife-grinder feeding cherubs / where do all the kisses go?

úterý

front-pages wordshipments, carving a non-stop itch / apples arent regulation, potato soil aint fake, cucumbers bend the colour scales / as for the bread dress—like nothing i've eaten before / a bit of primary heavy, drooling the most beautiful / thunder is its own true beat / lightnings sweet wannabe punk— sparks honey ma ears, and all the way and all-ways

středa

last walnut sun—and cream-light layered, the last cake / jsem anarchista, jsem anarchista, jsem / no apologies for over a week / swirl mocha strike up uncompromise beat / clear thunder of the hundred degrees / running with angelas wolves / you can huff and puff rumble-stiltskin but my marzipans safe / only tee-shirt possible : *sound-terrorist* orange on cornflower blue / *hail, hail freedonia* / instead for the old countries last court appearance tee-shirt kneading *kafka would've had a cow*—hoping for contempt / just ahead of the pack—there—little red / and riding never sweeter

scarif

barbwire unrolls the length of continent : wind playing those
low bass strings : how dust scratches (at) this dusk-drone.
husked pizzicato up against. and all this ... song ... as if life
depended—yours or anothers

rembetika : fado : tuareg guitar : tuvan throat : delta (u.s. or mekong)—each culture has their blues. bleed bluing longest clots of rust, deep-and-low. like casting nets—and in that almost/what?—whats almost there, what just slips through

like moths flagging and clagging up the night, heartbeats
mantling here and so in light. and in that festoon pursuit :
chase-leap-dodge, razor-wiring joint off thumb. more than
match struck, this is what salvation tastes? after a while they
reply, after a while

treatment resistant, a book swelled by damp. lengths of spine in gutters. a feather stranded cobweb, wind spiralling furious to unrelease. least the lark aint descending for now

torsos red sand baroque this doorway dance—night-gripped,
fear-heaved-dry—that much spark, don't speak, didnt, not. and
after? a globe of wire, sunflowers tooth-spit, was i being asked
to garrotte? but no—i'd misheard foxtrot

scar globs lower abdomen, hernia from lifting child, now
every time wanting to know why they cant fly. having to cut
pace-makers out before hitting the crem. sharp knives in the
washing-up rack—point uppermost

sheet glass, there, can you?—all haloed, world word leap. the
flicker of faces—the flicking of v's—the licking of wounds. salt
in gash before the crash; noise—this. take ma blood instead,
why don't? to witness the geometries of flame, fractals of blast,
nails-ice riven deep, scream my brother/sister, rip at hearts

rucksack station huge noise feet / insides a dress in butterfly
and perfectly / to right—wee lass and mother taking free seats,
their unbearable smiling on over. lasses hair in wee knots,
while her mothers are red braids. lass holds out handful of
fries, pretends to bite, shrieks with laughter. he could outsit
the stones, quieter than grass on a windless day, thats whats
razoring my mind. and the butterfly dress? his. terrified wearing
in his honour and ripping seams

is that a bruise or a tattoo?

where the sound is pebble-dash dash dash
pigeons whisper about a coup-coup
parcel delivery became logistics
spoon-rests got ergonomic
and bra-straps see-through
hammers held crookedly
pornographys actually read
and a minute erases all the clocks

the dawn chorus really doing my head in,
open windows, shouting the birds to stop
—their blind fucking optimism, wheres
all the conversations we've never had?

chips in curry
paper folded to
new transsexual
in 07980 and bold
     who attends
massage parlours
asking no extras
like ever?

marble-white butterfly
boogie-woogies
random beauty
inches from
briefcase n boots
quits while ahead
as calf-skinned board

the pissing-it-early-hours insomnia, opening door to your chipped-tooth *borrow some milk?* i'm bearing engels *condition of the working class in england,* 1845 open (no lie) to *social war is avowed and openly carried on*

fought with the milk-souring, with saucepans over-boiling,
with cartons tearing youve fought / fought with costume
jewellery crucifix ex placed round your neck, fought the bruises
rising and your panic rising / fought with the stairs and stars /
with doors and keys and shopping handles bust / fought with
fag-ash and smoke rings and burn patches ringing youve fought
/ all the wastelands silence, the paramedics and casualty youve
/ remotes and repair bills and tv licensing folk refusing to show
their i.d. youve fought / fought for the inches to be lopped
most of all youve fought youve fought for that most of all / and
won through, who'd of thought?

is that a bruise or tattoo?—there—
between your shoulder blades
the snake at base your neck

those with glass-hearts (shouldnt)
throw stones, you slip citrus to late pockets
wanting to peel you smell of oranges

chain tattooed round your ankle
apples around your hips
cant avoid being fucked to somewhere

switchback shimmy lips, latter-days
whistle blown, each canned heat and
sweetmeat freezing, clang steel

the dance floor, cock-ring speeding
puzzling faces, hit the door wide
the rest are bread-crumbs over empty beat

broken bottles are eyes on the street
the cctv of indiscriminate mouths
swallow-tattooed and wishboned

pubic hair like rolling tobacco
swimming pools need building
so tv's can be thrown

sky thin as dynamite
dreaming quick liquorice whip
in a ten pence pot of sherbet

strong as licit first kiss
first kissing in creosote dark
exploding lovehearts every shade

your heartsweet candyshop
fizzing tongues
unable to piss nights to come

happy hour is five to eight
the neon acid pink, all
rubbersequinfishnetfeatherboas
and half price lilies
—atlantis / stargazer / freakwiles

and all the young wanna
wanna be 18 again
sex flyposting
the largest selection
of cream cakes
a hole lotta shaking
the toast? in bronze
and arm in arming
keep your passage
honeymoon fresh

arizona is no the state i'm in and tho your tears have gritted ma
desert

                        i feel
                        i felt
                        that is
                        kind of
                        maybe
                        you know
                        you know   kind of?

fuck it must be hard enough growing up straight
        never mind this other stuff

starlings clenched black fist dead to gutter
fascists talk of colour when all blood is red

lovers discuss the most diseased animal
squirrel-pigeon-rat while jog-txt-coughing

faces hard as the municipal waterfall
grapefruit heavy as babys head

orange smile and seroxat anti-dee's hold-all
slipknots kicking out at clumsy pilgrims

g-strings tugged from bleached cracks
bling rimbaud would die for all over again

the rockabilly three giving it laldy
not blinking, attuned and in sync

until this rhythm-spill kid blows bubbles
her lustrous moons of hope

infecting us all one way or another
flickering through the big issue

see if youre still listed as
missing in action all these years on

the fucking dawn chorus doing me in
wheres all those conversations we never had

Lightning Source UK Ltd.
Milton Keynes UK
UKOW04f0257311215

265588UK00001B/49/P